PIANO SOLO

WILLIAM BOLCOM

NEW YORK LIGHTS

from
A VIEW FROM THE BRIDGE

Concert Paraphrase for Piano
by the Composer

EDWARD B. MARKS MUSIC COMPANY

EXCLUSIVELY DISTRIBUTED BY
HAL•LEONARD® CORPORATION
7777 W. BLUEMOUND RD. P.O. BOX 13819 MILWAUKEE, WI 53213

Commissioned by Premiere Commission, Inc.
for Bruce Levingston

NEW YORK LIGHTS
from "A VIEW FROM THE BRIDGE"
Concert Paraphrase for Piano

DURATION: 5:00

Libretto by ARNOLD WEINSTEIN
and ARTHUR MILLER

WILLIAM BOLCOM
(2003)

Stately; andante libero (stile d'una canzona napolitana)

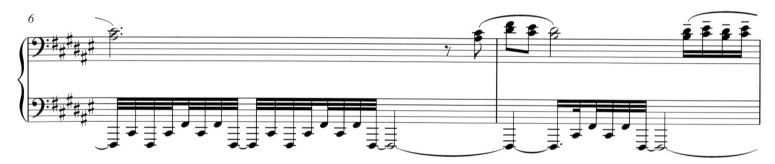

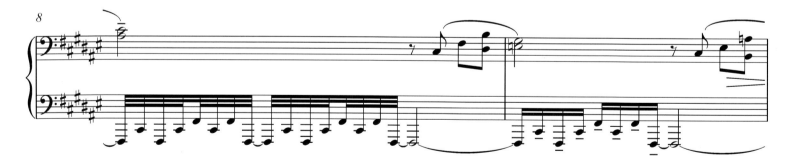

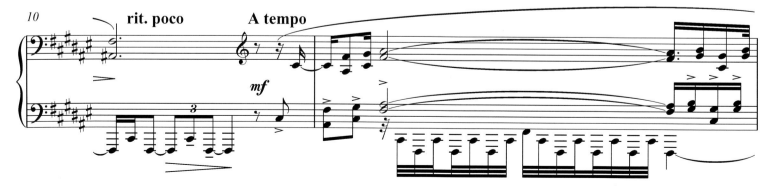

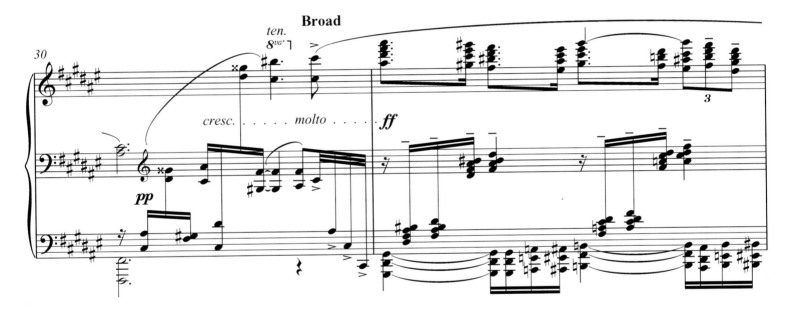

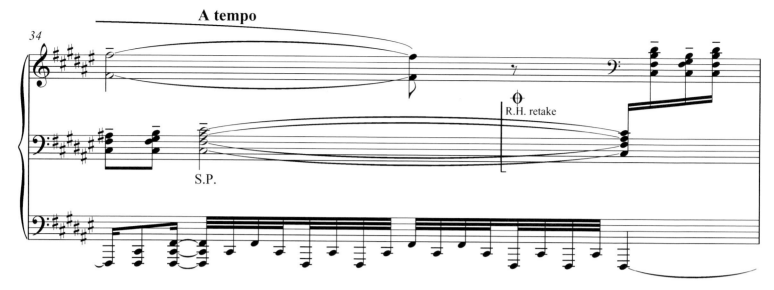

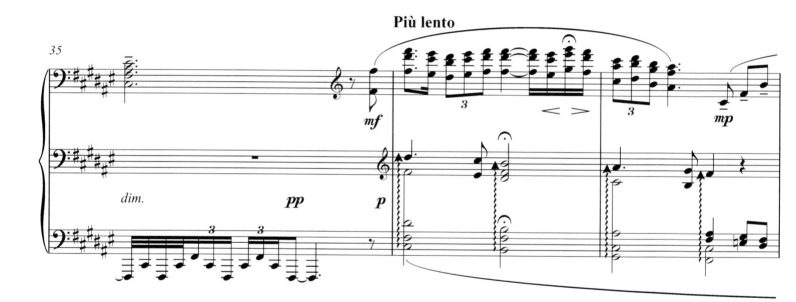

Nov. 15, 2003
Rome

U.S. $8.95

HL00220143

ISBN 978-0-634-09675-4